In the Distance

by

David Cooke

*For John
with all good wishes
David.*

David Cooke

David Cooke was born in 1953 in Wokingham, Berkshire, although his family comes from the West of Ireland. In 1977, whilst he was an undergraduate at Nottingham University, his poetry gained him a Gregory Award. His poems and reviews have been published widely in the UK, Ireland, and mainland Europe. A collection, *Brueghel's Dancers,* was published in 1984. After a long silence he has returned to writing. *In the Distance* reprints work which has long been unavailable alongside a generous sampling of previously uncollected work.

ISBN   1460965817
EAN   978-1460965818

All rights reserved. No part of this book may be reproduced or transmitted in any form or by any means, electronic or mechanical, including photocopying, recording, or by any information storage and retrieval system, without permission in writing from the copyright owner.

In the Distance is published by Night Publishing, a trading name of Valley Strategies Ltd., a UK-registered private limited-liability company, registration number 5796186. Night Publishing can be contacted at: http://www.nightpublishing.com.

In the Distance is the copyright of its author, David Cooke, 2011. All rights are reserved.

The cover images are the copyright of Douglas Robertson, 2011, and incorporate a photograph which is the copyright of Stephen Brindle, 2011. All rights are reserved.

Further copies of this book can also be purchased from any book store, or online at Amazon, B&N and other major online resellers, or by contacting abbeygatebooks@yahoo.co.uk.

Electronic copies of this book can be obtained from most major e-book retailers including B&N, Diesel, Kobo, iTunes and Smashwords.

Information about David Cooke and his work can be found at http://www.facebook.com/davidcookepoet

for Bernadette

ACKNOWLEDGEMENTS

I take the opportunity to thank the editors of the following publications in whose pages some of these poems have appeared or are forthcoming: *Agenda, Aspire, Assent (Poetry Nottingham), Bête Noire, The Big Little Poem Series, The Bow Wow Shop, Cannon's Mouth, Carillon, The Coffee House, Critical Quarterly, Cyphers, The Echo Room, Envoi, Foolscap, The French Literary Review, The Green Book, Grimsby Roads* (Edited by Peter Bennet, 1986), *Hibernia, Honest Ulsterman, The Irish Press* (*New Irish Writing*)*, The North, Ol' Chanty (Chanticleer), Omens, Orbis, Ostinato, Other Poetry, Outposts, Pennine Platform, Poetry and Audience, Poetry Durham, Poetry Ireland Review, Poetry Salzburg Review, Proof, Prole, The SHOp, Stand, Staple, Tadeeb International.*

Some of the poems were contained in a collection which received an Eric Gregory Award in 1977 and some were included in *Brueghel's Dancers*, which was published in 1984 by Free Man's Press Editions.

The lines by Nuala Ní Dhomhnaill from her poem 'Cathair Dé Bhí' in *The Astrakhan Cloak* are quoted by courtesy of The Gallery Press.

I would also like to thank those who on various occasions have given timely help and encouragement: Tim Roux at Night Publishing for his expertise and enthusiasm, William Bedford, Steve Brindle for his photograph, Patricia McCarthy, John Osborne, Ian Parks, Tom Paulin, Doug Robertson for his inspired artwork, Peter Robinson, Paul Sutherland, and my sister, Belinda, who for more years than I care to remember has been my sounding board.

Finally, and above all, thanks are due to my wife, Bernadette, to whom these pages are dedicated.

Generatio praeterit, et generatio advenit;
terra autem in aeternum stat.

One generation passeth away, and another generation cometh;
but the earth abideth forever.

Ecclesiastes

Is gan sinn tagaithe céim níos cóngaraí do Shliabh Shíón,
nó Cathair Dé Bhí, a Iarúsailim neamhaí.

And we've come not one step closer to Mount Zion,
or the City of God, his heavenly Jerusalem.

Nuala Ní Dhomhnaill

CONTENTS

Page

I BRUEGEL'S DANCERS

Bruegel	15
The Early Archaeologists	16
Hill-fort	17
Down	18
Visiting	19
Cows	20
A House in Mayo	21
Holidays	22
Easter 1966	23
Respects	24
The Morris Minor	25
A Ghrá	27
Epilogue	28
The Latin Lesson	29
Going to Mass	30
Churchyard	31
To My Father	32
Hospital	33
Memorial	34
After	35
Bistro	36
Four O'Clock	37
Jacob-Bellecombette	38
The Parcel	39
Route Nationale	40
House for Sale	41
Conveyance	42
Montesquieu	43
The Teatime Bulletin	44
In Response to Anger	45

	Page
An Elegy for Charlie Parker	46
Miles Davis	47
The St Kildans	48
Morning	49

II SLOW BLUES

Connacht	53
The Catechism	54
Schooldays	56
Luther	57
Pater Noster	58
Fathers	60
Ascendants	61
My Father the Pragmatist	63
Your Chair	65
Working Holidays	66
The Night Out	68
Gambler	69
Family History	70
The Gift	71
Occitan	72
Arnaut Daniel	73
Cathars	74
The Master Builders	75
Calvin's Geneva	76
The Rosetta Stone	77
The Season's Greetings	78
Krupskaya	79
For John Coltrane	80
Chicago's South Side	81
John Martyn	82
Slow Blues	83

	Page
Beyond the Humber	84
The Fortunate Islands	85
On the Front	86
In the Middle of the Way	87
Coda	89
Notes	93

I BRUEGEL'S DANCERS

BRUEGEL

There are times your dancers annihilate
the humanist in me, as in that northern
Cockaigne you viewed with a realist's eye
their heartiness tramps to raucous tuning.
The women are untouchable, blatant.
The yielding trestles are piled with plates.

And such lost revels what were they to you?
Did you celebrate, despise, or pity?
For there is shown mere lumbering daftness
as feet clump time on the floor. No heroes
of sentiment or ideal, they dance out
steps beyond all sins or goodness.

Yet here I see on one bleak canvas how,
primitive and docile, your six blind men
appall. Against a grizzled wash of sky,
a sparse landscape of church and trees,
they make their trek of faith: a procession
of pain from one dark ledge to the next.

Theirs is a suffering beyond reach
of plausible gods. Their desolate sphere
a bald despondent acre, here laid bare
to affront our safest minds. Blind sticks jerk
as they stumble on the bank of a stream;
while we tread the limits of what words mean.

THE EARLY ARCHAEOLOGISTS

Their patience an absolute they had fostered
on quaint erudition, they came to dig
the unsaleable tracts at the limits
of their own late empires: their vision too big
unless at last dust unleashed its secrets.

Polymaths and adventurers, whose faith
resided in biblical quotes and place names,
they tramped like prophets,
hoping their path would lead them to fame
once out of the wilderness of hunches.

Taking years themselves, they worked
through levels of time, disclosing
the chart of settlement heaped on settlement.
As methodology loomed to obsession
they sifted unglamorous fragments.

Dazed by the surge of dynasties,
a vast chronology swamps me, dims perspectives
whose light might fathom sand-locked eras;
leaves me pronouncing names on a list,
turning over the dross of eroded lives.

HILL-FORT

Evening, and small fields
are reapportioned in shadow,
the hills smudged dully
against a residue of sky.

The honing call of a curlew,
distant, is finally
no more than the sky's soft
pulse. Night draws in,

and the mind is a function
of its yielding light;
it makes out smoke
from a further camp,

the sense of it borne
upon a stirring of breeze.
I imagine dogs
and people, their utensils

ranged around fire;
the land burdened
with lumber of settlement;
blood-heat of habitation.

DOWN

On long afternoons at Johnsforth
I laid myself down and listened.

My ear to the ground, I sensed far off
a thunder of horses trapped –

my animals burdened with death
and the weight of the hills.

Now there is no way back
to the child or his visionary landscape

where the well is boarded up
and the Iron Age fort bulldozed flat.

VISITING
for my grandfather

When once, as a clean-kneed
child from town, I first came
on a visit to your limewashed
house, your two great fists

impressed me, for they
were ponderous chunks
of granite, notched
carelessly for fingers

and which, at your own willed
creation, you had torn
from the heart of the land.
Yes, I knew then how

you had risen and, separate,
must have kept on walking.
I was almost frightened
to be your friend, but still

am running so breathlessly
beside you as you stride
onwards, the castle of yourself,
across rough fields

of thistle and clover.
And the dogs are running
before us, and our laughter
creates again a flawless sky.

COWS

From compartment windows
they were fake, too far away
to be real. Friesians, shorthorns,
angus: painted cows

in a book of fields –
while on the train I rampaged,
shuttling impatience
through pages and pages

of green. Unexpectedly,
we'd arrive and land in a world
where they moped.
The first day up, a drover,

I'd goad them on with a stick
and then savour their warmth
at milking when packed
into pungent stalls,

where a white jet steamed
frothed up in a galvanized pail.
The fields outside
were full of their muck

in pats that were ringed
and perfect. Wherever
I ran that muck
would cling to my shoes.

A HOUSE IN MAYO

So long abandoned, their house and garden
lay caged in the tangle of briars. As a child
I looked for secrets, creating new lives
each visit from what they had left behind –

a cartwheel found in a shed with scraps
of chains and leather: disused tackle
they'd handled. One gable down completely,
I pictured thatch that the wind had blown.

And rain had weathered that house till it showed
a harsh perfection the owners did not see.
Around it their ordered plot ran wild
in a furious zone of growth and process.

Drawn to that absence, I explored it all
and forced a way through where tall weeds struggled
against me: the tough bright heads of ragwort
alive each summer in a haze of midges.

Empty houses were scars on the landscape.
Wild seeds blew in to heal them. When people
vanished, the tracks they had made were smothered.
Returning, all I ever found were mine.

HOLIDAYS

A treeless terrain,
it was neatly parcelled
by drystone walls
and ditches, mapped out

in identical townlands:
Carrickandy, Bohola –
names bright with
a garbled music;

and there I learned
I had senses –
the sombre reek
of turf stacked high

in a shed, or grass
laid down by a scythe.
Forbidden again
each summer,

I would climb up
to my grandfather's
hay, succumb
in its net of fragrance.

EASTER 1966
i.m. Peter McManus

On TV we were watching the soldiers
parade and saw, far away in Dublin,
how men filed past in martial splendour
while officials took a salute.

In droning celebration a band thumped out
The Foggy Dew. Did these heads, too,
drum to a bidding voice,
an identity: *Poblacht na hÉireann*

proclaimed in print across walls?
A die-hard republican veteran, you had shouldered
a gun in history. Fifty years later,
you were watching the screen with a child

and doled out lore and legend
in a steady tone of patriarchal
contentment. With an affable vehemence
you taught me that history was lived.

Memorial pageant, a smokeless sky –
we heard crowds cheer in Dublin.
In sprucened duds I can see you again
as you jauntily strut on parade.

RESPECTS

Her hand at the door, my aunt
said quietly: *He's going*
and then urged me in to speak.
Why? for I found him there
in desolate peace, beyond
all need of words or comfort.

Without will, broken,
he was propped up against pillows
and like a child had been bibbed
to feed. Sustaining nothing,
he slopped weak broth
from a bowl he could not handle.

Its warm breath flared.
It had no power that quickened in him.
I played a part ten minutes –
the quietness pounding its anvil –
and quit. My dying bones
were light as those of a bird.

THE MORRIS MINOR

A lustreless
black, it slept all night
in a shed with the relics

of a different era:
a crumbling harness,
broken tools, a horseshoe

nailed to the wall –
then gargled to life
on busy mornings

when we drove
into town or to Mass.
Down the lane

the old man nudged it
as it lurched on
wrecked suspension,

its bodywork
strafed by brambles,
until at last

he coaxed it out
onto the open road;
and all those trips

we made in convoy
across that rambling landscape:
Enniscrone, Pontoon and back.

So many kids
and so much lumber –
the whole bloody tackle!

A GHRÁ

The words for love
in a different language;
two syllables salvaged
in a slow decline.

Archaic welcome;
a vocative;
rug placed
on a chill stone floor.

A table set;
a fire;
dim lights
that ford a darkness.

EPILOGUE
for Belinda

Coonalingan and Johnsforth,
my terminal townlands –
when I take myself back
it's summer again:

the corn in stooks
like a redskin's village;
the swallows slicing
through miles of blue.

How easily then
we assumed our right
of entry where our books
and accent exclude us –

the snug interiors
where Christ's heart glowed
on a wall, delf ranged
on an ancient dresser.

Around the table,
foursquare, central, we sat
for soda bread, tea and cake.
Above our heads

from wedding photos
those who had left
smiled past, their features
fixed, yet distant.

THE LATIN LESSON

With sturdy jowls Brother Athanasius,
who back then we knew as *Beef*, chomped great slabs
of Virgil, which he digested for us,
struggling with the English in Brodie's cribs.

Aeneas and Father Anchises moved
through a pagan world obscured by the toils
of syntax, while we shambled on, reproved
by a voice more urgent than the Sybil's.

The Brothers could all quote Latin, pronounced
with a palatal blandness, the soft sounds
of a church's dialect, and enhanced
their wisdom with words unscholarly minds

found locked in lexicon, drill, declension.
And those words, too, were the smell of incense
in a quiet house of genuflection,
tall candles lighting the untouched presence.

GOING TO MASS

I shuffled at the back
for years, and kept a truce
at home by looking
at others around me –

the prim communion faces
worn like a mask
on dutiful daughters;
or those lighters

of candles, old women,
who crooned the response
from missals and knelt
as though caged

from doubt; through
pious circumstance
each rite had refined us
in faith, but now

when the host is raised,
a tiny weightless moon,
it drifts in orbit
beyond all touch of mine.

CHURCHYARD

With arms outstretched,
a Victorian angel
– its bald wings
hunched on shoulders

that have borne
the weight of years
of rain – faces out
my gaze in silence.

Stone upon stone,
its weathered squads
lie obliquely couched
in growth, endure

in this crowded
plot as the names
and the dates incised,
sparse legends

that made each slab
unique, are slowly
effaced to these barely
discernible scars.

No birdcalls here
can stir the dead,
no rote we intone
can reach them:

their voices dust
in quiet places,
their gestures dispersed
with broken stars.

TO MY FATHER
ave atque vale, Catullus

So I send these words out,
faltering, along an unlit path –
as if words now

could urge a ghost
to break its final silence,
terse enough whilst living.

Or what do I know
of the life you led
the years before I was born

when, with a minimal nostalgia,
you quit your Sligo outback
to skip through towns

in a country at war?
A potato-picking nomad,
a grafter, you biked flat miles

across the Eastern Counties.
Your son, and now
a father, too,

I have taken your place
to resemble you more and more –
born one country and a world apart.

HOSPITAL

Over and over his wife rehearses details,
awake all night, observing
the changing shifts, their faces.

Where air was pure
he lay at risk,
hooked up to clean apparatus –

Its routine *blip!* still
functioning
after his breath was spent.

MEMORIAL

In a windowless room they had laid you out
in a crisp white bed of linen.
Packed tight in a huddle around you,

we had entered to see you displayed.
Your body at rest like a saint's,
no awkward warmth or gruffness remained

to stir its monachal calm.
At one temple your hair had been shaved,
revealing the healers' scar. They had trimmed

the growth that darkened your lip
to an unaccustomed moustache.
A gathered clan we stood, each lost

in a separate silence
until the drone of a rosary began.
Like a long abandoned language

its monotone rose, familiar, to beat against
bare walls: a cycle of mysteries
that could explain or change nothing.

AFTER

In the musty aftermath
of last night's rain
and a sense of your body's comfort
I pace our room. Arranging books
or washing cups
I tidy away the morning.

Settling down to my table
this afternoon, too, will pass,
sifting listless pages,
while I hear again a sound of dogs
that miles away
through sleep were barking.

BISTRO

Crossing the road for a bar, we dance
through the headlamps of cars.
I open the door and the cold ignites,
your face aglow as laughing
we break a silence.

In the yellow light inside
the shiftless gather to decipher
their lives on a screen. Sitting down,
we order hot wine and a grog.
The *patronne* turns,
too sour to spare us a word.

When our drinks arrive
we sip at warmth from spoons.
Across a glaze of desert light
your face is a flood of smiles.

FOUR O'CLOCK

Again and again
I breathe through the surface

of sleep: an unretraceable
zone of comfort.

On a table beside the bed
my watch ticks on minutely –

its diminutive tattoo
filling out these empty hours.

Outside a shutter
bangs open and unsettles

the darkness near me.
It's four o'clock, I seem to say

as your restless face
drifts round,

hurt,
to ache in its nest of arms.

JACOB-BELLECOMBETTE

Up here at a height where you see
the surrounding mountains I forget my illness
and the arcaded streets below.
Beyond the level of roofs
the leaning cross on Nivolet
is pinning rock and air.

Here before its season,
a fresh light this morning
has scoured each jutting face
to a rarer tint of white.

Refining the mass of outcrop,
it has reduced mere bulk
to an image and left chill air
with all distinctions neat.

THE PARCEL

The first thing in the morning
we kiss then talk for a while.

The day is a parcel
wrapped up in your smile.

On the bedside table
I feel for my ring –

a lopsided circle
that contains everything.

ROUTE NATIONALE

The heat that summer oppressed us
as day after day we travelled along
a flat unbending road; and bleak utilities
hemmed it in all that dragging section.
Past petrol pumps and hangars
that were candy-striped, ablaze,
and compounds packed with tractors,
it urged us on to town.

The road was a scar on clean
terrain. Further off, beyond
slopes of pampered vines,
the mountains, white-capped,
soothing, were coolness glimpsed
through the gauze of distance.

HOUSE FOR SALE
after André Frénaud

So many others have lived here before
and woken up each morning in love
to a happy routine of chores,
their lives efficient as they moved
through each room, dusting,
or carefully placing a vase on a sill.
Each time they drew their water
echoes swirled round in the well.

Whoever they were they've gone
and the ivy spreads, neglected,
slowly obscuring the upstairs panes.
I still sense their traces –
here where tea leaves have left a stain
or where I find their small repairs.

CONVEYANCE

Making love in a house that now at last
we own, we ease a strangeness, move
towards possession of that warmth we know:
the kindness of sheets. Around us,
packed in boxes, lies the clutter of our lives.

In the morning and then for days
decisions will crowd the hours, as your plants,
my books, the records, are absorbed by empty
rooms. The stealth of days will astound us.
We will find ourselves at home.

MONTESQUIEU

The dog-days scorch Bordeaux. Behind closed doors
at a desk he sits, charting norms through a sea
of print. As reason discovers the laws
that define the natural good, history
is a world he surveys, its changing customs
till day lies buried in a stack of tomes.

And all around his own domain prospers.
His ordered vines, absorbing light, ripen,
grow fat in that calm his method infers.
With goodwill, too, the just state could happen,
though law was its necessary logic
underpinning both virtue and rhetoric.

Mild-mannered, generous, what charmed the minds
of a dozen cities were unassuming habits,
the lens of an understanding that blinds
with moderation: if the way man fits
each circumstance depends upon chance alone,
then only justice could be a touchstone.

In the salons they read a luminous prose,
and savour his irony, each stricture
softened by wit. Wearing ideas like clothes,
an elite parades disingenuous postures.
Beneath chandeliers their voices tinkle.
They are hairline flaws in priceless crystal.

With his books he sits, alone in the fort
of learning, and barters his sight for knowledge.
The Old Regime has crumpled. The retort
of the street will crush all measured language,
its philosophy honed down to technique,
the edge of a blade whose thinking is quick.

THE TEATIME BULLETIN

It's early evening and the TV set is on.
You lay the table and the children scream
as the fraying ends of day unravel.
Through the mayhem of boxes, bricks and cars
you enter a room with plates
where sounds of appetite assail you.

While relayed at a saving distance
there is news of war, a drawn-out violence
that now annuls some formalist's haven.
In a sealed off quarter of a dusty city
bodies lie where heat is hazing –
a postcard prospect with trees
and benches, a straggle of shops that frames
the square, its dry air cracks to a dull staccato
as hours away in that glimmering focus
events wash like waves
that break on a brittle shore.

The faces there are representative,
their features blurred to a cipher, and bodies
rot, unclaimed, slumped in a final statement.

IN RESPONSE TO ANGER

These tangled days when,
having to recognize in myself
a spore that is ineradicable,
darkening, I feel too spent
to make a botched amends.

And each day our children
possess you more and more
as you respond with love
that unlike mine has no need
to seem backhanded.

Skulking in my tent of words,
I'll wait for when the light
at its necessary slant
illuminates our garden.

AN ELEGY FOR CHARLIE PARKER

I can see you sitting in the yard at Reno's
where the Mob's tight hold makes dollars spin.
You are scuffling the dust, then homing in
whenever Lester launches his solos.

Or I see you breathe at the music's source
through a taped and battered alto. Through scale
after scale you soar, so egotistical,
obsessive, chasing sounds no ears endorse.

Later on the hipsters hailed you –
Benedetti and a crew of fanatics
who, trailing wires in cellar bars, left mikes
in place that hoarded every note you blew.

You had known from the start you'd never win,
even though your style became a language
for all. And Lester, too, had to share that rage,
that anger that sticks like pigment in skin.

MILES DAVIS

Your barest whisper at first suffices,
expanding slowly to an arc of sound;

each reticent phrase the horn releases
freights the air as a theme is found.

In dapper suits, expensive shoes,
you stand, your back half turned to a crowd.

Just give the pundits what they've paid for –
all the music you make, and time.

THE ST. KILDANS

Their photos soften the lines on windswept
faces, the indelible imprint of seasons.
They are ranged before me, The Bird People,
in a phoney pose for tourists, adept
at taking shillings from those who travel
in style to a rock the Atlantic stuns.

For so many years they have kept their pact
of silence, still smiling at us wryly
with a tolerant, incurious stare
behind which their isolation is perfect.
What primal trust sustained existence there,
knowing only the waves' dull history?

Before the intrigued arrived in steamers
from a world of bricks and big ideas
they had subsisted on meagre holdings
by eating the oily flesh of fulmars;
their harvest the cracking of skulls and wings,
their economy founded on feathers.

Slowly revolving around manse and kirk,
they had learned a zealot's unyielding law.
Subdued by the yoke of harsh religion,
strict observance undermined their work.
A punishing God wiped out their children
and gave that grief their patience was made for.

MORNING

Wrapped in the tang of the morning,
I stand at the edge of a stone quay.

Above my head a tilted sky
spills like a conjuror's hat, the air alive

with contending cries as day renews
to rowdy light and gulls inspect their cargoes.

Scraps thrown, offal, anything is what they consume;
and as if to exist were their only function,

their greed is a celebration
of what has willed them into flight.

II SLOW BLUES

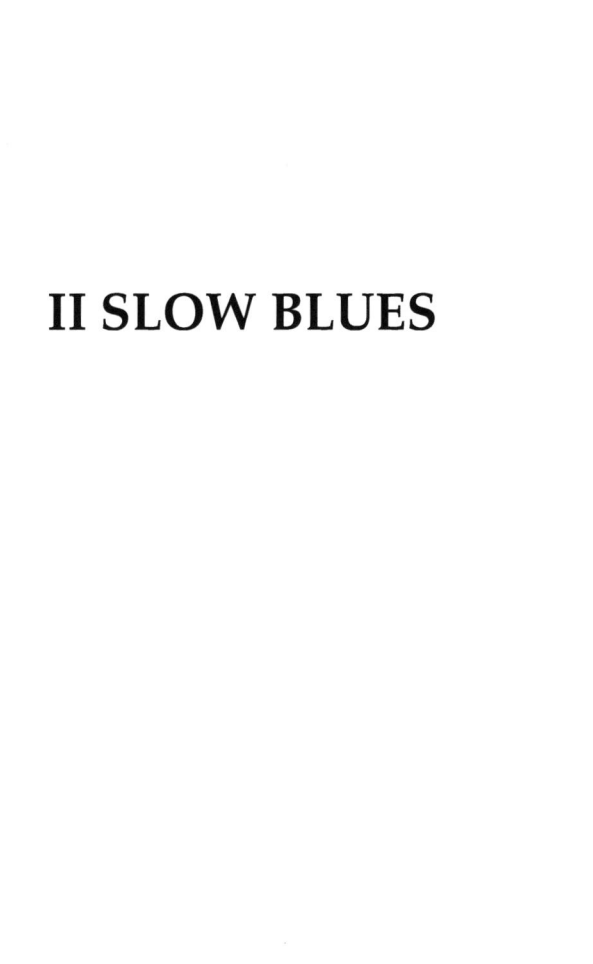

CONNACHT

Once again, I am homing in
on a landscape that is abstract
and generous, a photographic
collage whose cut edges merge
into the myth of perfect
childhood, a gloss of kinship;

till all our visits to country
cousins, whose lyric speech
made changelings of our tongues,
are now subsumed into one
floating summer, still
luminous above those hills.

An English nowhere could make
no claim on loyalty, when we left
behind each year its grid
of neat, pragmatic streets,
its ordinary day a dullness
that had shrugged off history.

How we hammed an identity
and hugged it close like homespun
before each death and marriage
unstitched its flimsy threads –
knowing now that Eden
is only a fierce nostalgia.

THE CATECHISM

Bored but efficient, I would learn
each week the allotted portion,
absorbing truths in easy stages
by courtesy of the CTS.
Who made you? God made me.

And why? as I paced to and fro
in my bedroom, intoning
like a mantra that singsong
of questions and answers
along with the rest of my work –

historical dates, irregular
verbs, the periodic table...
Knowledge was the gift
of the Holy Ghost. A mediaeval
rigour gave shape to the mind,

a taxonomy of virtues
and vices, as each drummed-in
certainty slid into place
like a block, a flight of steps
that aimed at the porch

of the Church Triumphant.
Just goodness wasn't enough
when even Socrates wasn't a saint.
Tridentine piety, a *credo*,
fenced in that perfect view.

I thought of Limbo babies,
and natives who had died
in darkness, though their lives
might be as blameless
as the sun on their unmapped sands.

SCHOOLDAYS

In our purple blazer
and gaudy tie
we sat: the putative heirs

to martyrs' blood –
though unlikely heirs
tuning in

to the back end
of the Sixties:
the philosophical

drone of Dylan,
slick blues
from Eric Clapton.

The miraculous, too,
our staple
as we pondered

the Turin Shroud,
its spooky
mystic reminder

of what truth
underwrote our lives –
a foot in both worlds,

like Padre Pio
we possessed the gift
of bilocation.

LUTHER

At school I was taught to think of you damned,
damned in a pit with the fallen angels.
Martin Luther: a name it was easy to conflate with *Lucifer*.

Years later, with a secular mind,
I am studying your face in Cranach's portrait
to see what calm the Northern Renaissance
might bring to your turbulent features –
irascible, yes, and blustering,
but who could outstrip you in self-contempt,
the knowledge that leads
to a choice that is existential?

And when the germ of conscience
ran to seed in a sprawl of discontent,
what could you do, but turn your back
on your own, as blooded boots
trampled the mud of a piecemeal nation?

For you servility was freedom.
Translating the Word, you carpentered psalms
from a rough-hewn language;
glossed epistles in a privileged light –
that light that I reject,
leaving me with what? A shiftless,
liberal outlook that would shrug itself free
from your murderous century.

PATER NOSTER

Our father which...
How mere form
defined the distance

from *Our father who...*
We would have gagged
on that one

recalcitrant pronoun,
such constancy
in our rituals.

Or should I admire
our passion
for exactness:

those dim,
theological centuries
when Church Fathers

dissected texts,
disputing clauses,
a single vowel?

The truly blessed
were unyielding –
they couldn't connive

to save their skins,
and shocked
pragmatic pagans,

who picked
their gods up
where they found them.

FATHERS

My imaginary shore glazed by visions,
fierce brink of intellect and punished sand –
Africa, where a jammed syntax loosens
to yield plain prose that the pure
might understand, the shrill province
a furnace where effete Latinity
is forged anew and each man's Word
thrives on diatribe, death-wish, sell-out,
the watery balm of reconciliations.

I think of Augustine wandering
the bleached streets of his indulgence,
his pleasures daily reduced to a scatter of bones
like a picked carcase the noon-haze whitens.
Imperatives sound his hunger,
and urge him on to pick up, read, and seize
those sanctioned truths –
a momentary thunder filling his mind
with the din of certainties.

ASCENDANTS
i.m. John and James Cooke

On parade in perfect step –
my father and my father's brother,
down some big street in Dublin,
where a breeze is freshening,
and the nineteen fifties
are loitering round the corner;
and even if I've no way now
of asking either how they spent
the day, or what claim
each felt he'd a right to make
on an open-handed future,
they are still sharp in Sunday suits
straight out of the movies.

Beyond that city I can just make out
a cramped, pre-electric house,
where shadows swarm each evening,
and then the lane unwinding
through a bramble-obscured neutrality.
But these two, like shrewd apostles
will leave for good a place
they'll later remember as *home*,
reiterating one simple text:
Self-help and Profit, a need for work
I'd like to think can't own me.

And now they inhabit an abstract
space to become such symbols
as I might choose to make them,
leaving much unanswered:
like who it was controlled
the shutter on that buoyant day.
A brother in Philadelphia?

– The disembodied voice
I heard on the phone years back,
who could have been my father,
or my London uncle, through
a hoaxing Yankee accent.

MY FATHER, THE PRAGMATIST

While scarcely political
in what you might term
the ideological sense
of the word, my father
acquiesced in the theory
that *the whole world
looks out for its own.*

Which meant that, not
unnaturally, when he came
to vote across the water,
he gave his terse
but unequivocal assent
to the British
Conservative Party.

A united Ireland,
of course, would have been
his preference, but that
was sentiment and not an issue:
no shillings rang
in a patriot's
empty pockets.

And I remember how,
when I was ten or eleven,
our family relived
his war: he'd sailed
through the night
and just made it,
pulling spuds in '44.

Driving round Newark,
Spalding, Boston, splashing out
on B & B, we bumped
into one of his cronies
in some fusty, derelict
snug, where your kids
could drink inside.

Dossing in barns,
biking miles, I think
they had both been happy
when they found what seemed
like a home from home –
if only the fields
had been a bit smaller.

YOUR CHAIR

After half a lifetime of early starts,
and a few fly years that made you money,
you finally softened round the edges
and eased back, prosperous, into your chair.

It's there in our mother's place: a threadbare
seat of judgment, battered in the mayhem
of a clattery open house, its wrecked guts
sagging, its two arm rests coming adrift.

And fixed immovably in that still centre
you watched the racing on TV, shushed out
our conversations, as Michael O'Hare's
gabble of names stampeded to its climax.

Another windfall? Or a better prize –
To know you were flush enough for losers
not to matter, in a different country
to have attained a gruff serenity.

That chair has hoarded the words you uttered,
and releasing them at times, as we make
our late decisions, can fill up a room
with some cagey, warm, and toil-inflected phrase.

Your chair is true north on a map of memory,
and points out paths, the sanctioned ways still worth
your approbation, the cuteness implied
in *Whatever would your father have thought?*

WORKING HOLIDAYS

All those years of it, the same
vague journey every place we went,
driving to work each holiday
in a choky, smoke-filled den
at the back of my father's Transit.
Life was the business of earning
your keep; no peace for a drone
in a house where you paid your way.

And each time my school books
were laid aside and the pencil-work
had ceased, it was back to early
starts, the strange renewal
of an intimate routine
as he poured impossible mugs
of thick stewed tea, turned out
a slithery half-cooked fry.

We'd wait together at the front
of the house for his driver
to bring the van, its diesel
engine roaring assertively
down the street. Inside,
they were studying form
in the *Mirror* and *Sporting Life*,
exchanging gargled judgments.

The steel doors slammed forlornly
and we were on the road once more.
If I closed my eyes I imagined
we could make it to the next
frontier, when all we did was land
on a creeping new estate
where opening up those doors again
my gaffer showed me the light.

THE NIGHT OUT
for Paul

Going upstairs, I can think of him still
in the bathroom, crooning. It's *Danny Boy*,
or some doomed melody dredged up
from a past we're unable to share.
Nearly all of the words are missing
as he tries half-heartedly to reinvent them;
while the tune gets sprightly,
pepped up for a night on the tiles.

When I played my records he told me
that music always needed a lilt,
a syrupy air you could hum
like a song of John McCormack's.
I was into the blues, the sax, significance –
No way my blacks or Dylan could *sing!*

His judgments were mostly like that:
definitive, unbending, like his sense of style
marooned in the nineteen fifties,
when the rest of us came along –
his wild locks restrained,
sleeked down with a blob of Brylcreem.

GAMBLER
Il faut parier, Blaise Pascal

Bound over for playing at pitch and toss
or, more portentously, *having gambled
on Her Majesty's Highway*,
my father was always an expert
at weighing up the odds,
made light of his brush with the law.
His gambling a science and pastime,
he never lost much, but knew
in the end that the world is flawed –
at best you could only break even.

He had taken us all to Ascot races,
and once took me to the Dogs,
where the speakers bounced
their fractured echoes,
the track suffused in lights
and where, with my own small bet,
so much depended on the hare's
mechanical, panicked blur.

Unschooled, he'd never read Pascal,
but knew what he needed to know
about risk, so went to Mass on Sundays.
The odds on heaven were evens.

FAMILY HISTORY

I
Piety, reverence –
what shall we call it,
the quiet we make
in the noise of living?
We place cut flowers
in a hollow stone:
what emblems,
what resonant words atone?

II
In the end our visits
become a ritual
as Christmas finds us
clocking up definitive
miles down motorways
to where his wife
keeps as busy as ever.

III
And our children now
are a kind of gift
we bring along to share:
two growing sons
who scarcely knew him,
two daughters he will never see.

THE GIFT
i.m. Peter McManus

Speeches from the Dock. It was just a book
that I never found time to read.
One summer, years ago, I picked up a copy
to leave as a gift for that affable, authentic,
old man who let us rule his roost.

Tall stories, fields, politics: his talk
was a warm anthology that told us
where we came from, that here it was
we belonged; that the past was names
enshrined in pages of a martyrology.

Wolf Tone, Emmet, Casement –
through his eyes I try to see them all again,
each shade impassioned, eloquent,
as they hold their accusers spellbound,
raw syllables streaming in a classical flood.

Our past was a landscape perfected
in memory, where each tree
is rooted, solitary and firm.

OCCITAN

Even language dies, its culture
reduced to signposts hoarding
stony fragments: Ribérac,
Carcassonne, Béziers and Montségur –

a scorched terrain once lit
by penitential fires,
where land-hunger and dispossession
were the mind of God imposing order –

enlightened vowels supplanted
by a graceless legalese;
and dabbling in that tongue
to tap a lyric source,

I heard the sound of a *planh*,
a keening note that rises
in Languedoc and Connemara.
I could see myself

once more, a bookish child,
deciphering a primal landscape
where Galway, Mayo, Sligo
were *Gaillimh, Muigheo, Sligeach*.

ARNAUT DANIEL

The women he courted, high-born, aloof,
played out their games with a deft
decorum, soaking up his praise,
though his craft was more
than a ceremony of dalliance,
a seasonal song to elaborate
on the violent arousal of green.

When spring lit up his South,
enlivening obdurate stone,
the cold halls of warriors,
his art was a special calling –
the debt he paid for the gift
of a chosen language:
his Roman tongue, its vowels
and consonants marshalled
in a strict, enduring music.

So Dante named him best of makers
when he placed him in Purgatory
for love, and forced his patience on
through each obscure gradation –
a slow refining that he, too,
might have understood, his image
for care the workshop,
his verses planed and filed.

CATHARS

Beyond the expedient, the flawed, the wasteful,
and the flames of their own purgation, ghosts
have risen, incandescent, into a clearer element.
Purity possessed them. Others, too: Tertullian,
enraged, twisting Latin into brutal periods,
a rhetoric of denunciation; or Trotsky, exiled,
his hair swept back, his mind clenched,
holding a pen, firmly, like a surgeon's knife.

THE MASTER BUILDERS

They made a prayer out of balanced stone,
the improbable height of a spire –
as if by risking Babel's curse
they'd glimpse the gates of a factual
heaven. The Truth was a presence,
palpable and massive, their skill
an arrogance made to serve it
with mathematical certainty.

In the shuffling parishes time
dragged, bogged down in the tick
of generations. Elsewhere
violence spragged the ordered fractions
of a working day, and trailed
behind it corpses, smoking fields
of discord getting nowhere.

Vanitas. Designs and frayed ambition
all that's new beneath the sun.
Pride, too, raised each edifice
above its echoing pit;
and took the measure of stone
and dressed it, hoisting it up
until it soared like logic
into the high, unanswering air.

CALVIN'S GENEVA

Like a theological Sparta,
I try to imagine his city state
secured against all doubt;

and a mind as poised
and incisive as a chill
sentence from Seneca.

There is a blue lake
for contemplation,
and sky as clean as a plain text

above its huddled streets –
a fundamental crisp air
that nips your breath like tonic.

As each small press grows loud
in the rattle of inspiration,
translations and tracts

gain ground, where tattered
fiefdoms coalesce
into the map of Europe.

But no truth here
is graced with ambiguity
as conviction wields

its flensing light,
peels back the stiff accretions
on a hand-me-down morality.

THE ROSETTA STONE

Curious, I read how in those wars
one side unearthed it, renewing
their defences, and think of sappers
standing there, intrigued
by a chunk of black basaltic rock
that their picks have cleared.

When all hostilities had ceased,
the tussle for antiquities began:
a defeated general laying claim
to *personal possessions*.
At length they shipped it here
to squat, unimposingly, amongst the spoils
of a still ascendant empire.

The Assyrian gates, ornate and ponderous,
or the paw of a couched, imperious lion,
spell out beyond ambivalence
the plain prose of power.
The stone kept them guessing.

It took Champollion to crack it,
who thought he had opened the book
containing all the answers.

THE SEASON'S GREETINGS

January, and a scurf
of weed maps out
the ducks' ornamental pond.

They trawl through
a pent Sargasso
past capsized bottles and cans.

Above each damp massif
of shrubs, where the spruce
and larch rear up,

a washed-out sky
denies transcendence –
its coldness a mirror

for the clenched,
ungenerous impulse
that dogs my steps today.

Another year blows in –
a beggarly wind from nowhere
snatching the trees' small change.

KRUPSKAYA

When I answered the letters Ulyanov
wrote me, I had guessed already
what love might mean: my attentiveness
a discipline to make me as pure
as our shared white exile,
our sweet talk sinking
into the language of a big idea.

The exhilaration! Like a troika ride
through candied forest –
the abruptly shaken manes of horses
scattering their halo of sound
until we are distant,
disappearing, reduced at last
to a quietness wrapped in tinsel.

And such contentment in possessing
only what we needed: our books, ourselves,
a purpose. Years later we visited
terraced slums, and then worked on
into a foreign night –
our homeless script like figures
tramping across the snow.

FOR JOHN COLTRANE

As over and over the same chords churn
your notes pour forth in spate –
sheets of sound erupting till harmony

is wrenched awry. When you sweated out
smack to cleanse your system,
your were hell-bent on an afterlife,

a body refreshed, believing.
You could call it Love, but sombre,
that force that drives you on.

Hearing you now, I feel reproved
for all the ways I lose my time –
books unread, the work I've left undone.

But your gift is a Fury;
it's like a disease,
the craving that makes you blow.

So who counts up the cost in pain –
the candy bars and cokes consumed,
your aching teeth clamped in the embouchure?

CHICAGO'S SOUTH SIDE
A photograph from the Thirties

In this picture of a Chicago slum,
snapped by a lens whose eager eye was sweet
on dereliction, there isn't a soul at home –
unless inside they've closed the doors
to exclude all trite concern.

Their silence hangs like the aftermath
of a long slow blues, when a single
crudely amplified note has bruised the smoky air.

No signs of life in their rubble garden,
unlit by the dreariest tint of green,
or flap of washing or tattered curtains,
disrupt an image of abject stasis.

Ground floor windows are boarded up,
and wires hang slack like obsolete rigging
against a colourless sky, where chimneys
balance, fixed in a rickety equilibrium.

Chicago, Detroit, New York –
big cities shine like easy money
at the end of a dusty rainbow.

JOHN MARTYN
i.m. 1948-2009

In the picture-perfect scenery of Challes-les-Eaux
in seventy-five, locked in private darkness,
I played your lost indefinable music
on a tired loop of tape: *Solid Air* –
its title track an elegy for a friend you couldn't save,
while you were destined to survive.
With a brawler's zest for living,
you absorbed the booze and heartbreak.

When I heard you had died I found you
in the afterlife of *YouTube*, restraining tears
for grief you'd caused,
knowing your muse, Serendipity,
had always been a harsh one, that even now
there could have been no easier way.

SLOW BLUES

And then there are afternoons
of exquisite boredom
when, record by record,
the classic scales subside,
and a voice rises
and the horn reaches
for the true note of lament.

This is the poetry
of a studious youth,
its song nudged by dissonance
towards those cleansed horizons –
the mythic home of the dispossessed.

BEYOND THE HUMBER
for Ian Parks

An immeasurable distance seethes:
ultima thule a blank frontier
where grey sky and grey sea
boil down to a blur of extinction.

You could wait forever here
for sirens' voices cheeping
a sugary southern song –
so no need now to block my ears
against the lilt of danger.

The heroes here were workaday:
trawlermen and whalers,
their mythology composed
of sweat and casual deaths,
hard graft on keel-roads.

Brought to this coast by chance,
I, too, must learn to live here now:
my collar turned to a wind
from the edge of the world.

THE FORTUNATE ISLANDS
from the Portuguese of Fernando Pessoa

What voice comes in the sound of waves
that isn't the voice of the sea?
It's the voice of someone speaking
who, if we listen, is silent,
and will not be listened to.

For it's only when half-asleep
we hear it, but are unaware,
that it speaks to us of hope –
makes us smile like a child asleep
while we, too, are dreaming.

There are fortunate islands
somewhere, lands beyond location
where a kingdom lies, waiting...
But when we awake there is silence,
and all we can hear is the sea.

ON THE FRONT

That bleak December sky, it's as cold
and unanswerable as the plodding logic
of doubt and schools our unkempt visions
in the levelling rigour of its light.

Taking my stroll this early evening
I walk past illuminations
that like the icons which haunted childhood
are dormant till night comes round again.

Today no cloudscape lures my eye
beyond this solid edge,
or hints at some lost home –
the domain of weird hierarchical choirs.

IN THE MIDDLE OF THE WAY

Reading again his verses in a language
I have yet to master, I deliberate
where syntax snarls as page by tangled
page I check my crib for meaning.
There is a straight path through it,
if I can work through detail,
and clearings lit by familiar usage,
their sound and sense fused and memorable.

So I start again from a dark wood
that bristles with analogies, though here
at least my text is clear: a solitude
where a dead poet still parades his fear –
a locus read until it's got by heart.
He struggled against a falsehood,
while I must stumble on words
he wrote to make his falsehood plain.

Who like him, too, now find myself
in the middle way: another June,
as the year clicks through a zodiac
that is for me a brittle image.
His putative planet brought him comfort.
His science misconstrued it.
My watery northern sun presages only
another fizzled English summer.

The middle of the way, and half-way
through the year: these are the tropes
I shuffle, seeking cadences of loss,
when for half my years a faith

like his sustained me, misremembered
scraps of knowledge that help me now
through footnotes, paraphernalia
of a poetry that's locked in time.

And if I've soused all that
in a sane Cartesian light, I know
what silt remains, what undertow of fear,
aspiring only to makeshift virtues
of decency and toleration,
a relativism that in the end
might damn my dithering soul
to the swarm-swept Hell of trimmers.

CODA

It seemed, suddenly, you had reached
your final period: like Beckett
endlessly inventing silences,
or Lady Day, her voice
reduced to a scorched whisper.

NOTES

Easter 1966: *Poblacht na hÉireann* is from the Irish Proclamation of Independence. It means *People of Ireland*. It is pronounced approximately as 'públucht na héhrun' with the 'ch' as in Scottish ' loch'.

A Ghrá: A term of endearment in Gaelic. It is pronounced approximately as 'a graw' with a very soft gutteral 'g'.

The Teatime Bulletin: The conflict referred to is the Salvadoran Civil War which lasted from 1980 to 1992.

An Elegy For Charlie Parker: Charlie 'Yardbird' Parker should need no introduction. However, I am indebted to Ross Russell's biography *Bird Lives!* (Quartet Books, London, 1973) for details about the life of this great musician.

The St. Kildans: This poem was inspired by a reading of *The Life and Death of St. Kilda* by Tom Steel (Fontana/Collins, London, 1975).

The Catechism: CTS stands for The Catholic Truth Society.

Schooldays: Padre Pio (25 May 1887 – 23 September 1968) was a Capuchin monk from Italy. He was venerated for his stigmata and was allegedly able to be in two places at the same time.

Pater Noster: The poem highlights the different ways the 'Our Father' was said by Protestants and Catholics in the 1960s when I was growing up.

Gambler: Given that God either exists or doesn't, Pascal suggested that Christian belief is a sensible gamble because there is little to lose and everything to gain. 'Il faut parier' means 'you have to gamble'.

Occitan: Occitan is the regional language of southern France. Very few people now speak it, although it was a major cultural language in the Middle Ages. A 'planh' is a lament. (The 'n' is soft like 'ni' in 'onion'). The Irish names are pronounced approximately as 'Gall-yuv', 'Mwee-oh', 'Shlig-uch' with the 'ch' as in the Scottish 'loch'. Arnaut Daniel: One of the 12th century troubadours. He was described by Dante as 'il miglior fabbro' or 'the better craftsman'.

Cathars: A religious sect considered heretical by mainstream Catholics in the Middle Ages. There was a ruthless crusade against them in the South of France.

The Rosetta Stone: The Rosetta Stone enabled Jean-Francois Champollion (1790-1832) to decipher the Egyptian hieroglyphics.

Krupskaya: Nadezhda Konstantinovna Krupskaya was the wife of Vladimir Ilyich Ulyanov, also known as Lenin.

For John Coltrane: After he kicked his heroin habit Coltrane was afflicted with a fierce oral craving.

In the Middle of the Way: The poem refers to a reading of Dante's *Inferno*. The 'trimmers' are those who sit on the fence or who, in the words of the Gospel, are 'neither hot nor cold'.

*

*Now as snowlight haunts the evening
I approach this buried village.
My other lives, my name, like footprints
that stretch behind me:
when more snow falls they'll cancel.*

Made in the USA
Charleston, SC
10 April 2011